7 Steps to Healthy Natural Hair

*written for Black women,
by a Black woman*

For information, contact Jazi Gifts by Michanna, LLC,

at 1-888-778-4808.

Cover Design & Photography: Michanna Talley

ISBN 978-0-6152-0984-5

7 Steps
to Healthy
Natural Hair

CONTENTS

Prologue

Some may ask the question, "What makes this woman an authority on natural hair?" Well, let me tell you. I have been 'au naturale' for about six years now. Like most Black women, I had my hair regularly pressed when I was a little girl, up until I graduated to getting perms every six weeks. I am very familiar with the 4+ hour salon experiences in an attempt to get my hair to do the opposite of what it was created to do. I initially wanted a perm so I could be like everyone else. Everyone else had a perm, so I wanted one too. My mom eventually allowed me to get one. My first perm experience went well, although I was very frightened that all my hair would end up on the floor. This did not happen, and thus began the every six weeks touch-up ritual. I always got my hair done at the salon, so I honestly cannot relate to those of you who have in the past or do perform the box perm kits at home. Even though my hair did not fall out during my first perm experience, it did come out in patches from time to time. When this occurred, I would temporarily stop getting touch-ups until my hair grew back. I had somewhat long hair, so as long as I wore it down, no one knew the difference.

After about four years, I could tell my hair was getting thinner and thinner. I would then shampoo my hair frequently (since the longer I went without shampooing my hair, the thinner it appeared). To sum it up, I blended in with and was part of the "straight hair club" all throughout high school.

Let's fast forward to college, more specifically, the prestigious Howard University in Washington, DC; as school began and I progressed as a college student, finding salons to maintain my straight hairstyle was slightly difficult. Just finding time to commit to having my hair "fried, dyed, & laid to the side," could be difficult. My hair also continued to become thinner and thinner. I eventually decided that I would no longer perm my hair. It helped that I had other friends who had also decided to embrace their natural self. Thus began my journey. (I must admit I had a "relapse" about 3-4 months in to growing out my perm, which caused me to once again begin the growing-out process.)

Initially, I would blow-dry my hair, which made the new growth straighten out a little and I would style my hair as if I was still getting a perm. (Prior to this, I did have my hair pressed a couple of times.) Eventually, this no longer worked and I started just putting my hair in a ponytail on top of my head while it was wet. My roommate at the time affectionately called it a strawberry (I guess that's kind of how I looked). That summer I had been natural for about one and a half years. By now, I was definitely frustrated with two very different textures of hair on my head.

One day while I was at home, following the shampooing of my hair, I took my hair, piece by piece, and cut off the straight pieces of hair from the curly/wavy hair. It did take me a while to get used to seeing myself with short hair, since that was brand new to me. My small afro was at first covered up daily with colored bandanas to coordinate with my outfits. Eventually, I mustered up the courage to begin wearing scarves as headbands and to let my little afro be seen. I continued to shampoo my hair and let it do what it was created to do.

During this time, I tried many products from various curl activators to different types of oils, shampoos, etc. After about three months, I finally found products that I felt brought out my hair's best qualities, and I still use these same products to this day. As my hair continued to grow, I graduated to new styles and currently I have gotten to the point where I can do many of the same hairstyles with my natural hair that I did with my permed and/or straightened hair.

Back to the question, "Why is she writing this book?" I am writing this book because far too many times, I have heard, "Can I touch your hair?" or "How do you get your hair like that?" This is something I hear about once a week. The latter of the two questions is even something I have heard at natural hair salons from stylists, who should be telling me what do with my hair, not admiring what I have done myself.

*   *   *

I feel that many Black women, who may want to wear their hair natural, think that it will take more time or their hair just "won't do that." I am here to tell you, that your hair can do many amazing things and contrary to popular belief, natural hair does not have to be more time consuming than straight hair. After all, your hair will be a lot healthier, and it will thank you for letting it be just the way God gave it to you.

Remember, God doesn't make mistakes; he gave you the hair that he

intended for you to have.

1

Black Hair Myths

So many times I have heard, "Oh your hair is cute, but my hair won't do that, you've got that good hair." To this comment I always respond, "Exactly what is good hair?" As you can probably tell, I cannot stand for Black people to talk about good hair because I know exactly what they mean. They are referring to hair that is wavy or straight and more similar to typical Caucasian hair. The use of this simple phrase reiterates the fact that we as a race still have a slave mentality. Why is it that we want and admire those things that are not like us? Good hair is hair that is properly taken care of, end of story!

Due to our ancestry, Black people have several different types of hair. Some have wavy hair, others have curlier hair, and some even have straight hair. When compared to all other races, Black people have the weakest hair, prior to any manipulation of our hair. When we perm our hair, we are breaking the bonds of our hair, making it even weaker. A lot of times, people don't perm their hair, but they do press their hair consistently. This too breaks the bonds of the hair, but it occurs at a slower rate than that of relaxing our hair. This is why some women who have never had a perm but have straightened their hair for years, can now do the same things with their hair as someone with a perm.

I have also heard from time to time, "My hair just won't grow." Well, we definitely know this is not true, just by looking at men and young boys with braids or individuals with locs. Their hair is still in its natural state. In addition, they do little with their hair and let it be. I am a firm believer that those who leave their hair alone as much as possible and work with what their hair was created to do naturally, have longer hair, than those who really strive to have long hair. These people many times revert to wearing weaves, getting braids with hair added, and torturing their hair on a regular basis. This goes back to the common belief that when you're not looking for something, it will come. When you are not overly worried about your hair, or how long it is, or trying to manipulate it further from its original state, instead of just trying to make sure it is healthy, it will grow.

Also, we as a people must not be scared to trim our hair. Hair is just that, hair. It will grow back. Trims are necessary. I am not one to advise you to trim your hair every six weeks like most hairdressers will tell you. You can tell when your hair needs a trim. Depending on how well you take care of your hair, you may not need a trim as often as someone who does not take good care of their hair.

Don't believe any of the negative ideas about your own hair. These notions have a history behind them and are one of many negative thoughts planted by others to further debilitate use mentally, making us think lesser of ourselves. The bottom line is, take good care of your hair, work with it and not against it, and we **ALL will have good hair**.

2

Products: What to Use & What Not to Use

In our current society, many people are becoming more and more conscious about what they are putting into their bodies. They pick up food products in the store and automatically turn them over, so that they can read the nutritional values as well as the list of ingredients. This is how we should be with our hair products.

There are three main ingredients that you should avoid at all costs; they are petroleum, mineral oil, and alcohol (any ingredient ending with –ol). This is mostly important for how you hydrate your hair.

Grease is primarily made up of petroleum. Instead of actually hydrating your hair and/or your scalp, it forms a film on top and does not moisturize. Therefore, grease gives an oily feeling, not true moisture, thus robbing your hair and scalp of the moisture that it needs.

I recommend that you primarily use oils on your hair. However, make sure that the oil that you choose does not contain mineral oil. Mineral oil has the same effect as petroleum. For this same reason, oil sheen is completely out of the question. As you can probably tell by now, many of the products geared for "ethnic" hair, as it is referred to in several stores, are not truly good for our hair but temporarily allow your hair to shine, therefore harming our hair in the long run, causing it to be more prone to breakage. (It is possible however to find products to give your hair a shine, but without forbidden ingredients. These products are usually in small spray bottles, unlike typical oil sheen products.)

The three forbidden products mentioned previously are slightly less important to look for when shopping for shampoo and conditioner, simply because these two products are rinsed out of the hair. When looking for shampoo, make sure that you stay away from clarifying shampoos. Clarifying shampoos are only going to strip your hair of all its moisture and cause it to be very frizzy. Look for products that are moisturizing and/or for dry hair. The same is true for conditioners. I personally use a moisturizing conditioner which, according to the label, is for permed, relaxed, and color-treated hair, of which I have none. Leave-in conditioners contain a lot of alcohol, so use very sparingly. The only time leave-in conditioners make an appearance in my hair regime, which occurs very rarely, is when I choose to blow-dry my hair (with a comb attachment).

This brings me to coloring your hair. Although I find coloring hair a nice way to get a different look or to change up your style, it is terrible for your hair, even when in its natural state. In order to obtain a major color change, our hair, due to its dark hue, has to first be bleached, and then colored. This bleaching step, once again, similarly to a perm, breaks bonds in our hair, causing it to be very fragile and prone to breakage, the opposite of what we want. I only caution you to color at your own risk!

Last, but not least, water....... For most women, water is considered "evil" when we think about our hair. As little girls, if we had our hair pressed, we stayed as far away from water as possible, avoided going outside when it was raining, not playing too much so we wouldn't sweat out our hair, and not daring to jump in a swimming pool during the summer. Your hair should never limit you from doing what you want to do. In reality, water is your hair's best friend. Water is a natural hydrating agent and once your hair is all-natural, water is truly your best friend. Your natural hair is also easier to style when it is wet. With natural hair, you too can step into the shower, not worrying about a shower cap, and let your hair get wet. I do not condone however, shampooing your hair everyday. As you already know, our hair needs a lot of moisture, and even though we can moisturize it ourselves, the daily natural oils produced by our scalp are very important. In addition to the natural oils, I also apply oil to my hair when it is wet or damp. This allows for the moisture to be trapped in, causing your hair to be hydrated and healthy.

Finding the right oil for your hair can also be trial and error. You have to find an oil that is not too light, and one that is not too heavy. A light oil will do no good in holding in moisture, while an oil that is too heavy can cause the hair to be stiff and lead to buildup. At times, you may feel that even though you are following your normal moisturizing protocol, your hair remains dry. When this happens, I recommend using a hot oil treatment. Which kind you use, is not necessarily important, although you should try to stay away from those with a lot of fragrance (sometimes labeled "aromatherapy"). You may need to purchase one or more of these. They are inexpensive (less than $2 each) and readily available in almost all beauty supply stores.

Just remember, stay away from petroleum, mineral oil, and alcohol.

3

Natural Hair Salons: To Go or Not to Go?

When I had relaxed hair, I very rarely shampooed and styled my own hair. I had a set appointment every two weeks at 4 PM on Wednesdays. When I went off to college, I was somewhat in a state of shock that I had to do my own hair, so... when I started wearing my hair natural, I thought that I would just revert back to my old ways and get my hair done on a regular basis. I have tried several different natural hair salons, and even though my hair looks nice when I leave, it is usually not so great that I want to return. In fact, I do not believe I have ever visited the same salon twice. Plus, usually even though the stylists claim to be natural hair stylists, their methods do not match this statement. Several so called natural hair stylists use small toothed combs and do not take time to properly detangle the hair. Natural hair is a whole different ball game than relaxed hair.

I mentioned before that I have had natural hair stylists comment on my hair and ask how I care for my own hair. This definitely rubs me the wrong way. They should be the experts, not me. I only work with my hair, instead of the variations that they get to see. In the end, the decision to visit a natural hair salon is yours.

Also, many women with natural hair wear "protective styles" such as braids, cornrows, or two-strand twists. I do wear these styles, but only about once or twice a year, when I want a small break from doing my hair.

Everyone is different, likes different hair styles, and has the time and money to invest into their hair. Do what is best for you. You know yourself and your hair better than anybody.

4

Basic Natural Hair Care

Natural hair cannot be cared for the same as straightened hair. For one, only use wide-toothed combs. I only comb my hair to detangle it while I have conditioner in it. All other times, I only finger-comb my hair. I do use brushes (with very soft bristles) very rarely when putting my hair up. Once you brush your hair, it may be harder to get your hair back to its curly state. Brushing the hair can also cause it to frizz. To block frizz, the easiest thing to do is to style hair while it is wet and then leave it alone. Try to use as little force as possible when styling hair (while wet of course) and DON'T TOUCH!

I have heard several different views on nighttime hair practices. For those of you who may blow-dry your hair or wear it out in a combed-out or picked-out afro, feel free to braid your hair into large braids at night and then cover with a satin/silk scarf. If you're like me, and wear your hair curly, wearing a satin/silk scarf seems to increase the curls and make them more separated and profound. Sleeping on a cotton pillowcase with no scarf will soak up all the oil within your hair, the opposite of what you want. For even more defined curls, try shampooing your hair in the afternoon or at night. Once you rinse out the conditioner, apply oil to the hair. LEAVE your hair alone and allow it to dry. Lastly, place a silk/satin scarf on your hair before you go to sleep. If your hair is not yet dry, you can use a blow-dryer (with no comb attachment). Most mornings I wet my hair in the shower. The more days past the hair shampooing day, the curlier and more defined my style becomes. (This practice may or may not work for you during fall and winter months. During this time you may choose to wear protective styles such as cornrows or two-strand twists.)

Here's a word of warning. Blow-drying your hair regularly (with a comb attachment) can cause it not to revert back to its curly state. The same is true for pressing your hair. I have friends who have had their hair pressed, only to have to cut off all their hair and start the growing-out process once again. After blow-drying my hair, it can take between two and ten different washes to get my curly hair back in its original form with little frizz (each shampoo is coupled by a whole day of air-drying). If you do choose to straighten your hair, let me suggest that in between your straightened or wavy hairstyles, or those hairstyles which require brushing the hair, wear a "wash 'n go" style for about a week to let your hair "recover." After a while, certain styles may take a toll on your hair.

An important lesson that I learned was to work with my hair and not against it. When exiting the shower, I usually shake my head and let the hair fall where it may. Once it does, I manipulate my hair only very little. If your hair does not want to do something, it will not, and if you force it to, it may not stay or look the way that you would like it to look.

What should you draw from this? **Work with your hair and not against it, with as little force as possible.**

"Tools of the Trade"

Wide-toothed combs

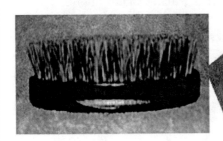

Soft bristle brushes

Headband,
Shoestring

5

Natural Hair – The Early Stages

When you first go natural, I believe this is the most difficult part of the transition. If you're anything like me, you are probably not accustomed to short hair. Not being able to put my hair in a ponytail was also a little bit difficult for me to get use to. However, looking back now, I wish I had treasured that time. This is a great time to figure out what works for your hair and what does not. Since the hair is short, it is a lot easier to wash out products that just are not working for one reason or another.

During this time, you will also get to know what your natural hair is really like, not what you assume it is like. As a young girl, before relaxers, my hair looked nothing like it does today. When I was little my mom would blow-dry and/or press my hair often. For this reason, my hair was "trained' to not curl. Bonds were slowly broken. During my initial natural experience, my hair did not curl at all. It dried similarly to a picked-out afro. Eventually, it began to curl, but not all at the same time. The hair at the back of my head began to curl first, which left me with a somewhat interesting look. Nonetheless, all my hair caught up, giving me a head full of curls.

Patience is important during this time. I am a true believer that hair can be "trained." Allow your hair to work its way back to its original state following years of abuse. Don't expect that you will cut away all relaxed hair and immediately have a head full of curls (like we see in the media). This is attainable, but it may be a process.

Enjoy the "short hair days" as I call them. Some find it easier to go through this stage during the summer, which is what I did, although not necessarily on purpose. Some of you may choose to remain at this stage. Know however, staying at the "short hair" stage may cause you to visit a stylist/barber regularly, to have your edges shaped up, for your hair will probably grow at a faster rate now that it is in its natural state. Those of you who want to continue to allow your hair to grow, read on.

Straight Hair Days

The Early Stage

my bandana days

6

Natural Hair – The Middle Stages

The "middle hair stage" was also the stage that I dreaded when I had relaxed hair. My hair was too long to be considered short and too short to put into a ponytail. The "middle hair stage" of natural hair however was not as dreaded, at least not for me. This stage was where I finally got completely comfortable with my hair as God gave it to me. If you make it to this stage, that says a lot about you. You have overcome the "societal brainwashing" that straight hair is best.

Around this time, my hair actually started to have defined curls (as noted previously). (Obtaining this is definitely a process. I suggest not blow-drying [with a comb attachment] or straightening your hair too much if this is the look that you want to achieve.) While your hair has grown by this stage, do not get caught up in length. Because our hair is naturally curly, you cannot really visibly see its true length. Your length can only really be seen in styles such as braids and twists (and sometimes not even then). If the braids or twists are done while the hair is wet, they will also shrink. Also, with your growing hair, you may come across tangles at your ends. Fight the urge to pull these knots. Invest in some professional or semi-professional shears and cut these knots out. If not, they can lead to split ends (of course attempt to detangle them first).

My everyday style during this time was an afro puff. When my hair was just long enough to achieve this style, I began by using scarves. I would place the scarf around the edges of my hair, tie with very little force, and then pull, and make a final tie when the hair had been pulled back far enough, to achieve the look I was going for.

Eventually, I got tired of trying to find scarves to match my outfits, so I started using black shoestrings to pull my hair back. I know this may sound a little crazy, but in actuality, this is a tool used often by many women with natural hair. I would use the shoestring in the same way as the scarf. After tying the string, I would use bobby pins to make it secure. This is a hairstyle which I wore religiously for about two years.

Even now, this is kind of a fall back style since it almost always looks good. You can also use elastic headbands instead of the shoestring or scarf, but the hair will only be pushed back a little and you will not necessarily have an afro puff, just an afro.

What you do with your hair before pulling it back is up to you. I would use a soft boar bristle brush to brush my hair all around the edges so that I would then have a smooth look leading up into my afro puff. You can also choose not to brush which will allow you to have a wavy look leading up into your afro puff. I will offer this word of caution for those of you who opt for the smooth look. Once you brush your hair, you kind of have to continue with this. Like I mentioned in a previous chapter, once you brush your hair, it will become frizzy unless it is pulled taut. If you no longer wish to wear the afro puff style, I would suggest re-shampooing your hair. Natural hair has a pretty good memory, and depending on what you do to it, it will not revert back to its natural styling until you shampoo it once again.

Protective Styles

Cornrows

Hair twisted while dry   Hair twisted while wet

Two-strand twists

Blow-dried

Shake 'n Go

Styles

ponytails made
with shoestring

with elastic
headband

afropuffs

wash 'n go
w/ headband

newly discovered
wavy style

7

Natural Hair – When You Have Arrived

This is the stage I have finally reached. It took me about five years to get here, but I made it. It will probably not take you this long since I cut my hair several times, which I now regret, but you live and learn. I personally say you have arrived when you can do with your natural hair the same styles that you did with it when it was relaxed. This is exactly how I come up with new hairstyles. I pay attention to those styles that everyone else is wearing, and then I do the same with my hair.

I do, however, still wear my "wash 'n go" hairstyle quite often. It has gotten a little difficult to wear this style as my hair is in my eyes since I just shake my head and let my hair land where it may. (More recently I had my mom cut bangs so that I could still just "wash 'n go".) My newest hairstyle is something I kind of happened upon. I have most recently found, that once I shampoo my hair, I put it into a low ponytail while wet. I wear my hair in this ponytail for about one to two days, to allow it to dry as much as possible. Once I take out the ponytail, my hair is in a wavy hairstyle that lasts for about three days. After these three days, it begins to lose its texture and shape. This style, just like any other, does seem to take a toll on my hair, so I only wear this style from time to time. Another cute hairstyle I suggest, centers around bangs. After shampooing or wetting your hair, shake your head and allow your hair to fall naturally. This will most likely land some hair in your face. Allow your "bangs" to hang as they wish. Pull back the rest of your hair and secure in a ponytail/afro puff. If you choose to place the majority of your hair in a low ponytail, allow it to dry, as mentioned earlier. Take out the ponytail and you now have curly bangs coupled with a wavy hairstyle.

Another aspect of this stage is your hair will probably become more time consuming. Shampooing and conditioning your hair will require more shampoo and conditioner, more time, and more patience. Ultimately be happy; this signals growth and healthy hair. You many also receive even more questions about your hair, such as, "Is it yours?"

Congratulations to those of you who have reached this stage. I also congratulate those of you who have opted to maintain a shorter style. Believe it or not, becoming comfortable with your hair, is coupled with becoming completely comfortable with yourself, natural hair, and all.

I've Arrived!

Epilogue

I hope you have taken a few tips from this book. If you are frustrated with your hair, don't be. Once you find those products that work for you, you will finally come to love your hair and cherish it as you should. I wish you all the best. And remember, there is nothing wrong with your hair the way that it grows naturally, just the way God gave it to you. We must start to embrace all those things that make us who we are, not those things that we have chosen to alter. Be yourself, work with your hair and not against it, and embrace your natural self.

If after reading this book, you still have questions, please direct them to:

StepsToNaturalHair@hotmail.com